Donald Trump

America's 45th President!

Have fun with facts, trivia, puzzles and more all about me and my job— President!

AGES 8 and UP

By Carole Marsh

Here & Now™
Things kids want to learn about today!

Senior Editor: Jon McKenna
Assistant Editor: Jessica Harton
Graphic Designer: Julie Green
Candidate Illustrations: Lee Barrow

Published by

GALLOPADE™
INTERNATIONAL

800-536-2438
www.gallopade.com

Gallopade is proud to be a member of these educational organizations and associations:

American Booksellers Association
American Library Association
Association of Booksellers for Children
Association of Partners for Public Lands
Education Market Association
Museum Store Association
National Council for the Social Studies

More by Carole Marsh

Here & Now
Learn about the 2016 Candidates: Hillary Clinton and Donald Trump Run for President!
The Republican Party Coloring Book
The Democratic Party Coloring Book
Political Parties and Elections Primary Sources Pack
Elections! Elections! Elections!: Fundamental Facts and Popular Projects for the Electoral Process
Presidential Elections Teacher Resource Book

1000 Readers
Barack Obama: America's First African American President of the United States
George W. Bush: 43rd President of the United States
William Jefferson Clinton: 42nd President of the United States
George H.W. Bush: 41st President of the United States
Ronald Reagan: All-American President
Jimmy Carter: The Nobel Prize President
Gerald Ford: 38th United States President
Richard Nixon: Expert on Foreign Relations
Lyndon B. Johnson: 36th President of the United States
John F. Kennedy: America's Youngest President

Biography FunBooks
Barack Obama Biography Funbook
Michelle Obama Biography Funbook
Sonia Sotomayor Biography Funbook
Thomas Jefferson Biography Funbook
George Washington Biography Funbook

American Milestones
Abraham Lincoln: America's 16th President
The Declaration of Independence: Quit Bossing Us Around!
The Bill of Rights: It Can't Be Wrong!
U.S. Constitution: Sign on the Dotted Line!
The U.S. Supreme Court: The Keepers of the Laws of Our Land

Carole Marsh Mysteries
The White House Christmas Mystery

Big Cool USA
Our Big Cool USA Activity Book
Our Big Cool USA Biographies Book
Our Big Cool USA Jeopardy Book
Our Big Cool USA Project Book
My First Book About Our Big Cool USA

A Word From the Author

For 228 years, Americans have had a great reason every four years to get really excited—a presidential campaign and election! Americans have debated with their friends and neighbors about who should be the next president, waited anxiously for the election, and eventually seen the inauguration of 45 presidents, from George Washington through Donald Trump.

The 2016 presidential election was extremely exciting! When candidates for president first started announcing in 2015 and early 2016, few people gave Donald Trump much of a chance. He had never held public office—in fact, he campaigned on the idea that America needed a Washington outsider! He also was very outspoken, and many Americans either strongly supported or strongly opposed his views and positions.

However, the Republican Party nominated Donald Trump, known worldwide for his real estate career and reality TV shows, as its candidate in July 2016. That launched a hard-fought election campaign through the fall, with Donald Trump opposed by the Democratic nominee Hillary Clinton, the former U.S. secretary of state, senator, and first lady. The two candidates energetically debated many issues that are important to the American people, from immigration policy to fighting crime to the best ways to add jobs or combat terrorism.

Eventually, the voters decided that Donald Trump should serve as the next president. He will be inaugurated into office in a ceremony in Washington, D.C., on Jan. 20, 2017 and succeed two-term President Barack Obama. Donald Trump has vowed to fill important government posts with people who will bring fresh new views to Washington.

This book gives you a great chance to learn more about Donald Trump and his presidential family. Every American needs to find out as much about his or her president as possible. That is part of being an involved citizen. And I hope you are looking forward to voting in your first presidential election—every vote counts!

Carole Marsh

4

Table of Contents

©Carole Marsh/Gallopade International/www.gallopade.com/Here & Now Series–Donald J. Trump

Hello, Mr. President!

Take a peek at Donald Trump's cell phone to learn more about our new president.

Donald John Trump

Date of Birth: June 14, 1946

Place of Birth: Queens, New York

Spouse: Melania Trump

Children: Donald Jr., Ivanka, Eric, Tiffany, and Barron

Grandchildren: Joseph Kushner, Arabella Kushner, Theodore Kushner, Kai Trump, Donald Trump III, Spencer Trump, Tristan Trump, Chloe Trump

Education: Fordham University (transferred 1966) University of Pennsylvania Wharton School of Business (graduated 1968)

Positions held:
• Real estate agent, The Trump Organization (1968-1971)
• Chairman and president, The Trump Organization (1971-present)
• Developer of prominent commercial office buildings, hotels, and golf courses in New York City, Florida, and California (1980-present)
• Host of the reality TV show The Apprentice (2004-2015)

6

Meet Donald Trump!

A presidential candidate is an ordinary U.S. citizen in many ways. Let's learn a little about me, Donald Trump—man, husband, dad, and grandfather! And, oh yes—PRESIDENT!

I love my Twitter account and usually send 12 tweets a day!

My favorite ice cream flavor is cherry-vanilla.

I style my own hair, but my wife cuts it.

I love See's Candies!

One of my most prized possessions is a shoe that Shaquille O'Neal took off after a game and gave to me.

My favorite movie is *Citizen Kane*.

I love spending time with my family.

My favorite lunch is a hamburger.

I scrape the toppings off my pizza...I do not eat the crust!

7

COOL DONALD TRUMP!

Music I Like...

Elton John,
Paul McCartney,
Michael Jackson

I like to watch...

Saturday Night
Live

Some favorite
books...

The Bible,
The Art of the Deal

Favorite phone...
I use both an
iPhone and a
Samsung Galaxy.

Some favorite
movies...

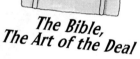

Citizen Kane; The
Good, the Bad and
the Ugly; Gone with
the Wind; GoodFellas

Hobbies...

Playing golf

Tweeting
(my Twitter handle is
@realDonaldTrump)

Spending time
with my
grandchildren

Driving when
I'm away from
New York

Reading
histories and
biographies

8

FASCINATING FACTS about DONALD TRUMP, Our New President

In 2007, I received the 2,327th Star on Hollywood's Walk of Fame! The star was for my role as producer of the NBC show *The Apprentice*.

In the 1980s, I helped develop "Trump: The Game," which is a board game similar to _____.
(*Answer is below right.)

My grandparents Frederick and Elisabeth Drumpf were born in Germany and changed their name to Trump after they immigrated to America.

I don't drink alcohol, and my favorite beverage is Diet Coke.

I attended the New York Military Academy and joined the varsity soccer, football, and baseball teams. I won lots of awards for my athletic performance between 1959 and 1964.

The Trump company brand spans a variety of industries and products, from real estate development to online travel and from ice cream to fragrances, just to name a few.

I have written 15 books that motivate people to achieve their personal and professional goals!

By the time I was 27, I owned 14,000 apartments through the Trump Management Corporation!

Rather than read e-mails on my phone or a laptop computer, I have my messages printed. I actually don't even have a laptop in my business office!

9

*Answer: Monopoly

Oval Office Occupant Oversees Official Orders!

The Oval Office is the most important room in the White House. It's where the president goes to work. It's where he or she meets with staff, visitors, heads of state, and signs bills and executive orders. It's called the Oval Office because of its oval shape.

Theodore Roosevelt moved the executive offices to the West Wing of the White House in 1902. The first "oval office" was built in 1909 and was located in the center of the south front of the West Wing. William Howard Taft was the first president to occupy it. Franklin Roosevelt enlarged the West Wing in 1934 and moved the Oval Office to its present location in the southeast corner of the wing.

Each president can decorate the Oval Office with his or her own mementoes, art, and furniture. He or she can also select art from the White House's extensive collection. Some presidents scattered family photos throughout the Oval Office. Others replaced the busts of Franklin Roosevelt and John Kennedy with busts of other former presidents. An oval wool carpet woven for the office in 1993, which features the full-color presidential coat of arms on a dark blue field, was once replaced with one in the southwestern shades of melon and sage.

President George W. Bush used the *Resolute* desk in the Oval Office. Queen Victoria of England gave the desk to Rutherford B. Hayes in 1880. It is made from the timbers of the *H.M.S. Resolute*. The crew of the ship abandoned it in the Arctic Circle in 1854. The desk was given to Hayes to recognize Americans' returning the ship to the British.

A bas-relief (a type of sculpture in which the design projects slightly from a flat background) of the presidential seal is on the ceiling. A portrait of George Washington, painted by Rembrandt Peale in 1776, hangs over the fireplace mantel (the same one that hung over the fireplace in the 1909 Oval Office). The U.S. flag and the president's flag stand behind the president's desk.

Trivia!
Many presidents have used the Resolute desk, but not always in the Oval Office. John F. Kennedy first used it in the Oval Office in 1961. Jimmy Carter, Ronald Reagan, Bill Clinton, and Barack Obama also used the Resolute desk in the Oval Office.

Trivia!
Other presidents used a "partners" desk, a desk with drawers on both the front and back which can be used by two people sitting across from each other.

Trivia!
President John F. Kennedy loved to introduce his kids to visitors. He would come out of the Oval Office and clap his hands, and Caroline and John Jr. (John-John) and their friends would come running. One famous picture of President Kennedy in the Oval Office shows John-John playing underneath his father's desk.

10

How would you decorate the Oval Office if you were president? Complete the picture of how your Oval Office would look! Color in furniture you would like, and draw paintings and photos inside the frames on the wall.

11

What Does It Mean to Be a Republican?

The Republican Party is one of two major political parties in the United States. It was founded in 1854 and is the second-oldest party still functioning in the nation. Republicans typically have more conservative views on economic and social issues than Democrats and want individuals, not the government, to solve these issues.

Why do we have political parties?

Decisions made by government affect us every day of our lives, and people have different opinions on how government should handle important issues. People who share the same opinions have formed groups called political parties that elect leaders to promote their ideas.

Both the Republican and Democratic parties have a symbol. The Republican symbol is the elephant, and the Democratic symbol is the donkey. Both were introduced in political cartoons in the late 1870s.

President Trump officially announced his candidacy for president on June 16, 2015, by issuing a press release. In that release, he said he would immediately make campaign visits to Iowa, New Hampshire, and South Carolina; and open a campaign office in New York City.

Famous Republican presidents include:

Abraham Lincoln

Dwight D. Eisenhower

Richard Nixon

Ronald Reagan

George H.W. Bush

George W. Bush

Former Indiana Governor Mike Pence will be his vice president. Mike Pence left his seat as governor to run for vice president, and he also previously served Indiana for 12 years in the House of Representatives.

In his announcement, Donald Trump vowed, "Quite simply, it is time to bring real leadership to Washington. The fact is, the American Dream is dead—but if I win, I will bring it back, bigger and better and stronger than ever before. Together, we will make America great again!"

Donald Trump:

The Path to the Presidency!

1. Donald's father, Frederick, groomed him to succeed in real estate. He worked for the family firm while he attended college.

2. In 1970, Donald joined the family business, then called Elizabeth Trump and Son. Shortly afterward, he led his first real estate deal to renovate a foreclosed apartment complex in Cincinnati, Ohio.

3. Donald moved to Manhattan, New York, in 1971 and started catching attention for bold architectural designs on larger construction projects.

4. An important event in Donald's business career came in 1986. He took over repairs to the famous outdoor skating rink in Central Park, Wollman Rink. The project was four years behind schedule, but Donald completed repairs in three months and came in $750,000 under budget.

5. In 2000, Donald entered the U.S. presidential race as a Reform Party candidate. He got more than 15,000 votes in the party's California primary. But he knew he did not have the backing of a majority of the party members nationwide, so he decided to leave the race.

6. In 2013, Donald decided against running for governor of New York. However, at the same time he did form an exploratory committee for the 2016 presidential race.

7. In June 2015, Donald formally announced he was running for president in a speech delivered from Trump Tower in New York City! He was chosen as the Republican Party's candidate at the party convention in July 2016 in Cleveland, Ohio.

8. On November 8, 2016, Donald was elected America's 45th president!

WHO CAN BE PRESIDENT?

Not everyone can become president of the United States of America! Both Donald Trump and his opponent, Hillary Clinton, had to be qualified to seek the office.

According to the Constitution of the United States, there are three qualifications to be president. The candidate must be a "natural born" citizen of the U.S, be at least 35 years old, and have lived in the U.S. for at least 14 years.

Trivia!

Women have always been eligible to be elected president; in fact, Hillary Clinton was the sixth woman to run.

The 20th Amendment to the Constitution states the vice president is to become president if the president dies. When William Henry Harrison died after only 30 days in office, Vice President John Tyler became president. At that time, it wasn't clearly stated in the Constitution that the vice president would become president, just acting president. Both houses of Congress had to pass resolutions declaring Tyler as president.

Trivia!

The Constitution doesn't say whether a man or woman is eligible. It only says, "No person except a natural born citizen. . ."

The 25th Amendment allows the president to nominate a new vice president if that office becomes vacant. Congress must approve the nomination. Harry Truman had no vice president after he became president when Franklin Roosevelt died. When John Kennedy was assassinated, Lyndon Johnson became president. Johnson did not have a vice president until he ran for election in 1964. The 25th Amendment allowed Richard Nixon to nominate Gerald Ford as his vice president after Spiro Agnew resigned.

©Carole Marsh/Gallopade International/www.gallopade.com/Here & Now Series–Donald J. Trump

THE DATE TO
INAUGURATE
IS JANUARY 20

Donald Trump will repeat the Oath of Office of the president of the United States on Friday, January 20, 2017. The ceremony will feature lots of pomp and circumstance, and a parade. Most of the country's most important federal politicians will attend.

"I do solemnly swear that I will faithfully execute the office of president of the United States, and will to the best of my ability, preserve, protect, and defend the Constitution of the United States."

Until the 20th Amendment to the U.S. Constitution was approved in 1933, presidents were inaugurated on March 4. The Constitution didn't set a specific date for presidents to take office, but our founding fathers meant for the president to assume power on the day the Constitution went into effect—March 4, 1789.

The first inauguration, however, didn't take place until April 30. Bad winter weather made travel to New York City difficult for congressmen (they had to count the votes). The votes for president weren't counted until April 6, and George Washington still needed time to travel to New York from his home in Virginia.

The 20th Amendment set Inauguration Day on January 20, two weeks after the Senate certifies the votes of the Electoral College. If January 20 falls on Sunday, the president takes the oath of office privately that day and again in a big public ceremony on Monday.

Interesting Inaugural Information

Franklin D. Roosevelt was the last president to be inaugurated on March 4 (March 4, 1933) and the first to be inaugurated on January 20 (January 20, 1937)!

Chief Justice William Rehnquist administered the oath of office with the same Bible used at George Washington's inauguration. The same Bible was used to swear in Warren G. Harding, Dwight D. Eisenhower, Jimmy Carter, and George H.W. Bush (George W. Bush's father)!

Thomas Jefferson was the only president to walk to and from his inauguration and was also the first to be inaugurated at the Capitol in 1801.

Warren G. Harding was the first president to ride to and from his inauguration in an automobile in 1921.

Ronald Reagan's second inauguration in 1985 was held privately on Super Bowl Sunday and then publicly the next day.

15

Donald Trump and the Great Debates!

Over the past few months, I was active on the campaign trail. I gave lots of speeches, appeared on TV, and debated with the other Republican candidates and then with Hillary Clinton.

Pretend you are a reporter at a White House press conference. What question would you like to ask me, Donald Trump, about how to improve education at schools like yours?

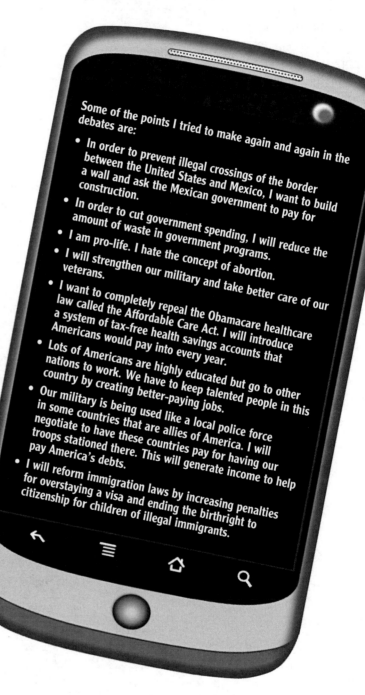

Some of the points I tried to make again and again in the debates are:

- In order to prevent illegal crossings of the border between the United States and Mexico, I want to build a wall and ask the Mexican government to pay for construction.
- In order to cut government spending, I will reduce the amount of waste in government programs.
- I am pro-life. I hate the concept of abortion.
- I will strengthen our military and take better care of our veterans.
- I want to completely repeal the Obamacare healthcare law called the Affordable Care Act. I will introduce a system of tax-free health savings accounts that Americans would pay into every year.
- Lots of Americans are highly educated but go to other nations to work. We have to keep talented people in this country by creating better-paying jobs.
- Our military is being used like a local police force in some countries that are allies of America. I will negotiate to have these countries pay for having our troops stationed there. This will generate income to help pay America's debts.
- I will reform immigration laws by increasing penalties for overstaying a visa and ending the birthright to citizenship for children of illegal immigrants.

16

DONALD TRUMP'S COOL WIFE!

It is said that "behind every successful man is a strong woman." I would definitely say that about my wife.

I first met my wife, Melania, in 1998 at a fashion industry party in New York City. I asked for her number, but she would not give it to me. Thankfully, she took *my* phone number and called me a few days later. We married in 2005, and our son, Barron, was born March 20, 2006.

Melania was born in what is now Slovenia and studied architecture and design before becoming a model in Paris and Milan. For the past nine years, she has been a stay-at-home mom for Barron. In 2010, she launched her own jewelry line on QVC. I am so proud of all her accomplishments!

When Donald first told me he was thinking about running for president, I said to him, "You cannot just talk, you need to go and run – and if you run, you will win." He has my full support because he is fair. No matter who you are, a man or a woman, he treats everyone equal. This makes him a great leader. He is not a typical politician, but that's what America needs.

I decorate and design the interior of all of Donald's properties, including the Trump Towers.

I'm choosing not to go political in public, because that is my husband's job. I'm very political in private, when it is between me and Donald. I know everything that is going on.

I speak six languages: Slovene, Italian, English, French, Serbo-Croatian, and German.

I make sure that Barron spends quality time with Donald. I see to it that Donald and Barron golf regularly.

Circle three things you think are most important for a good president:

EXPERIENCE   A TEAM OF HELPERS

EDUCATION   GOOD IDEAS

ENERGY   COMMUNICATION SKILLS

17

Who Are Those Kids in the White House?

Four of Donald Trump's five children—Donald Jr., Ivanka, Eric, and Tiffany—are adults who will not live in the White House. But 10-year-old Barron will accompany his parents to the White House.

Unlike a lot of boys, Barron does not mind wearing a suit and tie. His mother says he is not crazy about wearing sweatpants, though!

In his parents' penthouse in New York City, Barron had a whole floor to himself. What would you do with that much space for yourself at home?

_____

Donald Trump Jr.

Ivanka Trump

Eric Trump

Tiffany Trump

Barron Trump

Some of the youngest children to live in the White House were President John F. Kennedy's kids. His daughter Caroline was 4, and John Jr. was just a baby. John Kennedy Jr. liked to hide under his father's desk in the Oval Office!

When their father was first elected president, the Obama girls were the youngest residents of the White House since Amy Carter arrived in 1981. What was Amy Carter's father's name?

_____

Tad Lincoln was 7 years old when he moved into the White House. He liked to tie a chair to his two pet goats and have them drag him around the house! Do you know the name of Tad's famous father?

_____

Amy Carter had a special treehouse on the White House grounds!

President Teddy Roosevelt's children had many pets, including a pony named Algonquin. Roosevelt's son Quentin once brought the pony into the White House to visit his sick brother. The horse actually rode up the elevator!

18

See pg. 40 for answers

Donald Trump and the People Who Have Influenced Him

When I was growing up, I had the opportunity to become anyone I wanted, much like you do! Two men had the biggest influences on my becoming the person I am today.

Frederick Trump, my father, was heavily involved in New York real estate and introduced me to the business. He was fiercely ambitious and worked seven days a week to support my mother, my four siblings, and me. I remember my father inviting me to watch him at work after I completed my homework and on the weekends. He believed the best way to teach his children about the world was to let us watch it unfold.

A few times, my father came under scrutiny from the press and public. He was accused of bribing public officials to get real estate development projects, but never charged with a crime. I saw him stand his ground and fight for his family and his self-made fortune. He never took "No" for an answer, especially from his children!

Sgt. Theodore Dobias was my baseball coach at the New York Military Academy (NYMA). As the next generation of Trumps, my siblings and I were expected to behave, but I was a little bit of a troublemaker in elementary school. I enjoyed arguing with my peers and teachers, and sometimes the disagreements got out of hand.

My parents agreed I would be sent to NYMA for my teen years. NYMA was known for making bullies more gentlemanly and for toughening up weaker boys. While at NYMA, I met my next role model.

Sgt. Dobias was a combat veteran of World War II who saw action in some of the bloodiest battles in Italy. Our NYMA baseball team's motto was "Winning isn't everything, it's the only thing!" He was tough as nails, rough, and demanding, but we won nearly every game and I came to admire him.

Sgt. Dobias was always able to capture our attention and inspire us to fight or play until we won. He taught me to value power, strength, and winning.

These two role models shaped me into the man I am today. With my father's real estate knowledge and Sgt. Dobias' strength, I developed into a powerful businessman, politician, TV star, author, and Republican president.

Who are your biggest role models?

The Secret Service

Protecting the President and His Family!

The Secret Service was created on July 5, 1865 by the Treasury Department to find, and stop, people who were making counterfeit currency. It wasn't until 1894 that the Secret Service began part-time protection of the president. In 1901, Congress asked the Secret Service to provide protection for Theodore Roosevelt when he became president upon the assassination of William McKinley. By 1902, the Secret Service had assumed full-time responsibility for protection of the president.

The Secret Service protects the president and vice president and their immediate families. They also protect former presidents and their spouses; children of former presidents until age 16; visiting heads of state and their spouses; official representatives of the U.S. performing special missions in other countries; and major presidential and vice presidential candidates, and their spouses, within 120 days of the presidential election.

In addition, the Secret Service still investigates counterfeit money in the U.S. and overseas, credit card fraud, computer fraud, and financial institution fraud. They also investigate people who make threats against the president or anyone they are protecting.

The curved wire that agents wear around their ear connects to a special radio that lets them communicate with other agents. Civilians cannot hear the Secret Service communications. A surveillance kit is part of an agent's radio. It contains a microphone and earpiece. The kit lets agents keep their radios on their belts, so their hands are free while they work.

Secret Service agents agree to "take a bullet" for the president, which means they will defend the president's life with their own, if necessary. They agree to do this because they believe in our country and democracy. When John Hinckley Jr. tried to assassinate President Ronald Reagan in 1981, Special Agent Tim McCarthy was also shot. McCarthy recovered from his injury.

The Secret Service does use some special equipment to protect the president. The fleet of presidential limousines have bulletproof glass and armor plating to protect them, and their passengers, from explosives.

> The Secret Service Uniformed Division protects the White House, vice president's residence, and embassies.

Sometimes when you see pictures of the White House, you see men on the roof. They are members of the Secret Service Counter Sniper Team. Their job is to stop any long-range threat to the president. They have specially built rifles and special equipment to help them do their jobs.

> Secret Service agents wear sunglasses to keep the sun out of their eyes and so they can watch the crowd. Agents buy their own sunglasses.

> The president is also referred to as POTUS—Secret Service shorthand for President of the United States.

> Counterfeit currency is fake money people make on their own and try to spend like it is real!

> The Secret Service has code names for everyone they protect. President Trump's code name is Mogul. What would you like for your code name?

_____

> The Secret Service uses dogs from Holland, a breed called Belgian Malinois, to look for bombs. The dogs and their handlers have to finish 20 weeks of training before they can begin working.

20

Midnight Snacker

Protecting the President and His Family!

President Trump decided in the middle of the night that he was hungry. His Secret Service detail did not see him as he walked down to the White House kitchen to make a peanut butter and jelly sandwich. Help the president's Secret Service detail find him in the White House kitchen.

START

FINISH

21

Meet the Vice President!

**My name is Mike Pence.
My birthday is June 7.**

My name is Mike Pence. I met my wife at a church service. She was playing guitar, and I told her I wanted to join the group!

I have described myself as "A Christian, a conservative, and a Republican, in that order."

My parents ran a string of gas stations in Indiana.

Before I was elected to office, I worked in radio broadcasting. My conservative talk show was syndicated across Indiana!

In 1991, I wrote an essay for a magazine in which I admitted I was wrong to let some of my past political campaigns get too negative.

My wife and I have a son, Michael, and two daughters, Charlotte and Audrey.

I thought about running for president in 2016 myself, before I decided against it and then agreed to be Donald Trump's running mate!

My favorite flavor of ice cream is Moose Tracks! My favorite movie is *The Wizard of Oz!*

I ran for Congress twice unsuccessfully before I was elected to the U.S. House of Representatives in 2000. After six terms in Congress, I was elected governor of Indiana in 2012!

22

What Does the Vice President Do?

The major responsibility of the vice president of the United States is to succeed to the presidency in the event of death, resignation, removal, or incapacitation of the president.

Primarily, the vice president serves as the president's representative and carries out any duties the president assigns. The vice president also serves as president of the Senate and has the power to break tie votes in that legislative body. After a presidential election, the vice president presides over a joint session of Congress to certify the official vote count of the U.S. Electoral College.

The daily role and function of the vice president depends on the specific relationship between that person and the president. Duties often include serving as spokesperson for the administration's policy, advising the president on important decisions, hosting foreign dignitaries, and representing the president at special events.

Spokesperson: a person who speaks for or represents a company, organization or other person

Throughout the history of the United States, nine vice presidents have advanced to the presidency upon the death or resignation of the president.

Teddy Roosevelt was the youngest vice president to become president. He became president at age 42 after the assassination of President McKinley. The average age to become vice president is 53.

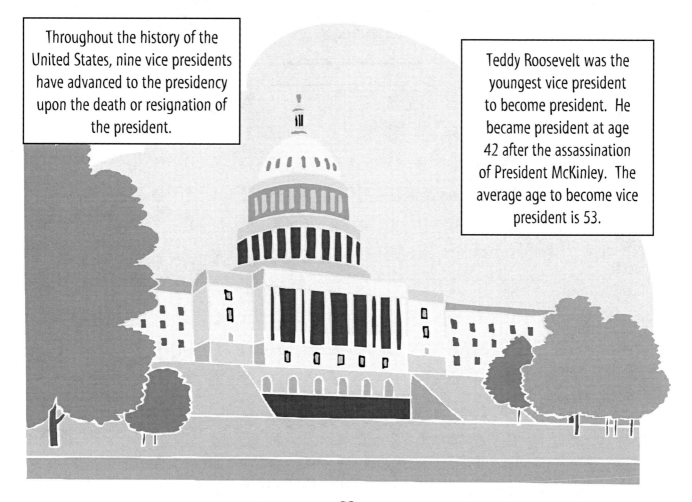

23

Serious About Succession

If neither the president nor the vice president can serve, the order of presidential succession is as follows....

- the Speaker of the House
- President pro tempore of the Senate
- Secretary of State
- Secretary of the Treasury
- Secretary of Defense
- Attorney General
- Secretary of the Interior
- Secretary of Agriculture
- Secretary of Commerce
- Secretary of Labor
- Secretary of Health and Human Services
- Secretary of Housing and Urban Development
- Secretary of Transportation
- Secretary of Energy
- Secretary of Education
- Secretary of Veterans Affairs
- Secretary of Homeland Security...

.... whew!

Word Search ACTIVITY!

Find and circle the words listed to the right of the puzzle.

Remember to cross off the words in the list as you find them!

T	S	B	I	B	U	X	Z	Y	A	Q	N	C
P	N	W	I	Z	D	T	I	F	V	R	P	O
S	R	E	S	O	L	U	T	I	O	N	R	N
U	E	A	D	V	E	G	G	B	M	A	E	S
Y	K	C	J	I	W	A	L	X	M	N	S	T
S	F	T	R	A	S	A	D	E	O	E	I	I
M	G	I	U	E	R	E	N	Y	T	Z	D	T
R	Y	H	L	U	T	D	R	O	R	I	E	U
S	A	K	T	A	M	A	F	P	D	T	N	T
X	P	A	Q	E	U	F	R	U	E	I	T	I
Z	N	P	N	E	S	Q	B	Y	B	C	D	O
D	Z	T	E	L	I	G	I	B	L	E	I	N
T	X	N	D	V	B	W	V	V	H	A	E	V

constitution
amendment
president
natural born
citizen
vice president
secretary
qualify
eligible
resolution

The Great Capitol Cabinet Conundrum!

Cabinets aren't just in your kitchen! I'm having a meeting with some of my cabinet members. Vice President Pence put numbers on the seats for each department, but didn't write my people's names on them!

I need your help, America! Help me seat President Trump's administration by matching the department's seat with its responsibilities. Just write the proper seat number in front of the department description on the list below. Thanks!

1 Secretary of Agriculture

2 Secretary of the Interior

3 Secretary of Defense

4 Secretary of State

5 Secretary of Labor

6 Secretary of the Treasury

7 Secretary of Veterans Affairs

8 Secretary of Commerce

9 Secretary of Housing and Urban Development

10 Secretary of Health and Human Services

11 Attorney General

12 Administrator of the Environmental Protection Agency

13 Secretary of Homeland Security

(a)_____ Department that serves as attorney for the government and its citizens, and enforces drug, immigration, and naturalization laws

(b)_____ Department responsible for our nation's public lands and natural resources

(c)_____ Department concerned with housing needs, fair housing opportunities, and improvement and development of the country's communities

(d)_____ Department responsible for controlling pollution

(e)_____ Department of the government most involved with people; duties include mailing Social Security checks and making sure health services are available

(f)_____ Department that assists veterans and their families

(g)_____ Department that helps improve farm income, helps to curb hunger and malnutrition, and helps landowners protect the soil

(h)_____ Department that serves as a financial agent for the U.S. government and makes coins and bills

(i)_____ Department that helps Americans who need and want to work

(j)_____ Department responsible for providing military forces to protect our country

(k)_____ Department involved in international trade, economic growth, and the advancement of technology

(l)_____ Department that advises the president about foreign policy

(m)_____ Department that takes precautions against terrorism

25

See pg. 40 for answers

TRAVELING IN STYLE
Top Priorities When Presidents Travel!

When President Trump needs to travel, he has a choice of limousine, helicopter, or a Boeing 747-200B aircraft.

The Secret Service won't say how many presidential limousines there are, but they are all designed to protect the president's life, wherever he or she goes.

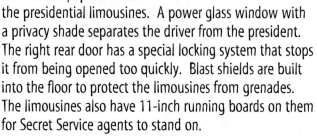

The presidential limousines are armored and customized Cadillac vehicles. The Secret Service calls the vehicle "The Beast." Instead of a television and a refrigerator, you will find telephone and radio equipment inside the presidential limousines. A power glass window with a privacy shade separates the driver from the president. The right rear door has a special locking system that stops it from being opened too quickly. Blast shields are built into the floor to protect the limousines from grenades. The limousines also have 11-inch running boards on them for Secret Service agents to stand on.

The presidential limousines don't have guns mounted on them, but the Secret Service agents are all armed. The limousines are usually followed by SUVs carrying Secret Service agents with automatic weapons.

The mission of the Executive Flight Detachment of Marine Helicopter Squadron One (HMX-1) at Quantico, Virginia is transporting the president wherever business takes him or her. The squadron has four different helicopters used to fly the president. When the president flies in one of these, it is called "Marine One."

Before any planned presidential flight, the crew members have a rehearsal flight to the site to make sure "Marine One" is mechanically sound. The rehearsal flight gives crew members time to fix any problems before the president gets onboard the helicopter.

When the president is onboard one of the two Boeing 747s that provide air transport for the president, the plane is called "Air Force One." The 89th Military Airlift Wing at Andrews Air Force Base in Maryland is responsible for Air Force One.

The flying "Oval Office" in Air Force One includes a conference/dining room, quarters for the president and spouse, and an office area for senior staff members. Two galleys (kitchens) can provide up to 100 meals at a time.

Today, the Trump family can travel in presidential style. Which travel option would you prefer—limousine, helicopter, or airplane?

Presidents started traveling by air in 1944. Franklin D. Roosevelt flew in a C-54 Skymaster called the "Sacred Cow."

President Harry Truman flew on the "Independence," a DC-6 Liftmaster.

President Dwight D. Eisenhower's planes were the "Columbine II" and the "Columbine III."

The call sign "Air Force One" was classified during the 1950s. It identified the president's plane, and when he was aboard.

JUST CALL HIM...
THE COMMANDER-IN-CHIEF!

One of my duties as president of the United States is to serve as commander-in-chief of all American military forces! As commander-in-chief, my duties include defending the United States during wartime and keeping the military strong during peacetime.

The president appoints the top military officers and helps decide what size the military needs to be. Appointments to top military jobs must be approved by Congress.

According to the U.S. Constitution, only Congress can "declare war" (to formally and officially state that the U.S. is at war with another country). However, the president can send American troops to other countries where the conflicts may be like a war, but war hasn't been declared.

Only the president can decide if the military can use nuclear weapons. The only president to make that decision was me, Harry Truman. To put an end to World War II, I ordered the military to drop atomic bombs on Hiroshima and Nagasaki in Japan in August 1945. The Japanese surrendered on September 2, 1945.

MATCH THE BRANCH OF THE ARMED FORCES WITH THE JOB IT DOES:

1. ARMY

2. AIR FORCE

3. NAVY

4. MARINE CORPS

5. COAST GUARD

____ **A** all the warships of a nation, with crews, supplies, shipyards, and officers

____ **B** the branch of the armed forces that protects the coasts, stops smugglers, and helps ships in trouble

____ **C** the branch of the armed forces trained to fight on land, sea, and air

____ **D** the branch of the armed forces responsible for the aircraft for air warfare

____ **E** a large group of soldiers trained for war, especially on land

27

See pg. 40 for answers

THE WHITE HOUSE
A HOME WITH HISTORY!

President Donald Trump and his family will enjoy living in the White House. Did you know the White House celebrated its 200th birthday in November 2000?

President George Washington and Pierre L'Enfant, the city planner for Washington, D.C., chose the site for the president's residence—1600 Pennsylvania Avenue. A contest was held to find a builder. Irish-born architect James Hoban submitted the winning design and received a gold medal for his work!

The cornerstone (the first stone laid at the corner of a new building where two walls meet) was laid in October 1792. It cost $232,372 to build the house. President Washington never lived there!

Trivia! *Recreational facilities for the president and his family include a tennis court, jogging track, swimming pool, movie theater, billiard room, and bowling alley.*

John Adams was the first president to live in the house, and it wasn't finished when he moved in in November 1800. The walls hadn't been plastered, and the main staircase wasn't finished. During the last 200 years, many additions have been made. The house has 132 rooms, 35 bathrooms, 412 doors, 147 windows, 28 fireplaces, 7 staircases, and three elevators!

Over the years, many first ladies have made improvements to the White House. The first rose garden was planted in 1913 by Woodrow Wilson's first wife, Ellen. John F. Kennedy's wife, Jackie, redecorated the White House and asked private individuals to donate antiques and artwork to the White House.

The White House has had many names. It has been known as the "President's Palace," the "President's House," and the "Executive Mansion." Because of the nearby red brick buildings, the white-gray sandstone house was soon nicknamed "White House." In 1901, President Theodore Roosevelt officially named the president's home the "White House."

The president's family lives in the center part of the White House. The Oval Office (the president's office), Cabinet room, press room, and staff offices are located in the West Wing. The first lady's office, and other staff offices, are in the East Wing. When a new president is inaugurated, the White House is refurbished practically overnight. By the end of the inaugural parade, the White House family quarters are ready for the new president and his or her family. The first family can decorate their private quarters any way they like. They can bring their own furniture, books, and artwork.

Trivia! *Running water was piped into the White House in 1833.*

Trivia! *Electricity was installed in the White House in 1891.*

Trivia! *The White House is the only private residence of a head of state open to the public, free of charge. Around 6,000 people visit the White House every day.*

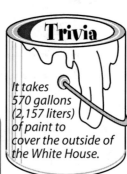

Trivia *It takes 570 gallons (2,157 liters) of paint to cover the outside of the White House.*

Trivia! *The White House kitchen has five full-time chefs who can serve dinner to 140 guests and hors d'oeuvres to more than 1,000.*

Now turn to page 29 to take a White House quiz!

WHITE HOUSE QUIZ

Questions and Answers About America's Most Famous Home!

1. When was the cornerstone laid for the White House?
   - a. 1800
   - b. 1901
   - c. 1812
   - d. 1792

2. What recreational facilities are located in the White House?

   _____   _____

   _____   _____

   _____   _____

3. How many rooms are in the White House?
   - a. 15
   - b. 132
   - c. 150
   - d. 250

4. Who was the first president to live in the White House?
   - a. George Washington
   - b. Theodore Roosevelt
   - c. John Adams
   - d. Thomas Jefferson

5. Where does the president's family live in the White House?

   _____

6. Which president officially named the White House?
   - a. Franklin Roosevelt
   - b. Herbert Hoover
   - c. Theodore Roosevelt
   - d. John F. Kennedy

7. When was electricity first installed in the White House?

   _____

8. How many fulltime chefs work in the White House?

   _____

29

See pg. 40 for answers

WHERE AM I GOING TODAY?
Top Priorities When Presidents Travel!

Hey kids! I'm going to be traveling a lot next week, and I need to figure out how I'm going to get to all these places! But right now, I have a meeting with my Cabinet—and I can't be late! I need your help: Take a look at my schedule below and circle the best mode of transportation to each destination. Oh, and if you could label the proper places on the map below, I'd really appreciate it!

DAY	ACTIVITY	FROM	TO	MODE OF TRANSPORTATION		
Monday	Attend Session of Congress	White House	U.S. Capitol	Car	Helicopter	Air Force One
Tuesday	Meeting with Governor of Virginia	Washington, D.C.	Richmond, VA	Car	Helicopter	Air Force One
Wednesday	Get Award in My Home Town	Richmond, VA	New York, NY	Car	Helicopter	Air Force One
Thursday	Tour Forest Fire Disaster	New York, NY	Blairsden, CA	Car	Helicopter	Air Force One
Friday	Meet with Prime Minister of Canada	Blairsden, CA	Ottawa, Ontario Canada	Car	Helicopter	Air Force One
Saturday	Throw Out First Pitch at Atlanta Braves Game	Ottawa, Ontario Canada	Atlanta, GA	Car	Helicopter	Air Force One

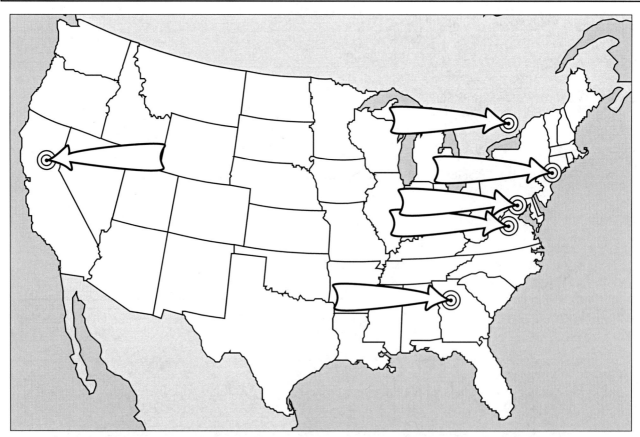

CAMP DAVID
A Great Place to Relax!

Camp David is a 134-acre (54.23-hectare) retreat for the president and his family and guests. It is located in the 10,000-acre (4,047-hectare) Catoctin Mountain Park, near Thurmont, Maryland.

The government bought the land, which had rough terrain and eroded soil, in 1936 with plans to turn the area back into productive land. The New Deal's Works Progress Administration (WPA) and the Civilian Conservation Corps (CCC) worked together to create the Catoctin Recreational Demonstration Area in 1939. Camp Misty Mount was built and first used by the Maryland League for Crippled Children. However, the area around Camp Misty Mount was too hard to negotiate in a wheelchair, so a second camp was built, Camp Greentop. During the winter of 1938-39, Camp Hi Catoctin, a third camp, was built for use as a family camp for federal employees.

Trivia!
Many historical events have taken place at Camp David—the planning of the Normandy invasion during World War II, discussions of the Bay of Pigs situation with Cuba in 1961, the Camp David Peace Accords between Israel and Egypt in 1979, and many discussions with foreign dignitaries and world leaders.

When Franklin D. Roosevelt was president, he spent weekends aboard the presidential yacht, the *Potomac*, or in Hyde Park, New York. During World War II, the Secret Service worried about the president's safety while he was on the yacht. So, they looked for a cool place in the mountains near Washington, D.C. Camp Hi Catoctin was chosen after President Roosevelt visited it in April 1942.

Trivia!
President Eisenhower had a bomb shelter built at Camp David that is located 65 feet (19.8 meters) underground!

President Roosevelt renamed the camp "Shangri-La" from James Hilton's novel *Lost Horizon*. Harry Truman called the retreat the summer White House. In 1953, Dwight D. Eisenhower renamed it Camp David to honor his grandson, David.

The main lodge at Camp David was made by connecting four cabins and is named Aspen. President Trump and his family will enjoy spending time there!

31

Donald Trump: Where Does He Stand?

Start Here

Every voter is interested in how a presidential candidate feels about important issues affecting America. Let's ask Donald Trump!

What will you do about relations with China and Russia?

Where do you stand on taxes?

I will renegotiate trade agreements with China. I hope to improve relations with Russia but only from a position of strength.

I want to give middle class Americans tax relief and reduce the headaches Americans face in preparing tax returns.

How will you handle illegal immigration?

What about healthcare?

How will you help people get jobs?

I will strengthen our borders and require employers to hire American workers first.

I will bring manufacturing that has gone overseas back to America!

What about government spending?

What about energy?

We must have available healthcare options that are affordable and well-administered, so citizens have freedom of choice!

I will cut the wasteful spending in the government.

Between natural gas, oil, solar, wind, and nuclear energies, we will give America energy independence.

©Carole Marsh/Gallopade International/www.gallopade.com/Here & Now Series–Donald J. Trump

ELECTORAL COLLEGE *versus* POPULAR VOTE

Why doesn't the person with the most votes win?

> When our country was founded, some leaders wanted the people to go to the polls, cast their ballots, then count each individual vote for president. The candidate with the most votes wins the election. That is called the "popular vote."

Others felt that Congress should elect the president. The Constitutional Convention of 1787 rejected that idea, because attendees felt the president would be controlled by the legislature.

As a compromise, the convention agreed on a method of indirect popular election, which eventually became the Electoral College.

> What is the Electoral College? It is the group of representatives chosen by the voters of each state, and Washington, D.C., to elect the president and vice president. The number of electors from each state is the total of the number of representatives and senators in Congress (all states have two senators).

For example, Virginia has 11 representatives and 2 senators. So, Virginia has 13 electoral votes. Vermont has 1 representative and 2 senators, or three electoral votes.

There are 538 electors in the Electoral College. To win the election, a candidate must receive 270 electoral votes. Candidates who receive a plurality (the highest number) of a state's popular vote usually receive all of a state's electoral votes. However, only 25 states, and Washington, D.C., are required by law to cast their votes according to the results of the state's popular vote.

The Electoral College meets in December to vote. The votes are sealed, then sent to Washington, D.C.

The votes are counted in January at a joint session of the House of Representatives and the Senate.

If no candidate receives 270 votes, the state delegates to the House of Representatives choose the president

and the Senate chooses the vice president.

> *Since the 2010 census (an official count of the population), the number of electors in some states changed. Ten states lost representatives, while eight states gained representatives. These changes were all due to population changes in each state.*

Presidential Pets

🐾 More than 400 "First Pets" have lived at the White House! Some of them include:

🐾 George Washington owned a horse named Nelson and several farm animals, but he did not actually live in the White House. Why not? It wasn't built yet!

🐾 John Adams owned the first presidential pets—two dogs and a horse—that did actually live on the White House property!

🐾 Abraham Lincoln owned rabbits, Jack the turkey, and two goats. Mr. Lincoln even let the goats run around the White House!

🐾 Theodore Roosevelt and his children had a lizard, a bear, a guinea pig, a badger, a pig, and a blue macaw parrot.

🐾 Franklin D. Roosevelt had Fala, a Scottish terrier.

🐾 Jimmy Carter owned a dog named Grits.

🐾 Bill Clinton had two pets, a dog named Buddy and a cat named Socks.

🐾 George W. Bush had Ms. Beasley, a Scottish terrier, and India, a cat.

🐾 Barack Obama adopted a Portuguese water dog, which his daughters named Bo, during his first presidential campaign.

Trivia!

Americans love pets. More than half of families in the United States have at least one pet. Pets are important family members.

Trivia!

U.S. presidents have had many pets—cats, dogs, ponies, even macaws and raccoons. Nelson was the first official "First Pet". He was the beloved horse of General George Washington, the first U.S. president. Nelson carried General Washington to victory at Yorktown—the battle that ended the Revolutionary War.

Trivia!

 Popular U.S. pets include dogs, cats, horses, fish, birds, snakes, ferrets, turtles, hamsters, gerbils, and guinea pigs.

Trivia!
President Abraham Lincoln let his pet goats, Nanny and Nanko, ride with him in his carriage.

WRITE ABOUT IT!

Pretend your father or mother was the president. Write a diary entry of a typical day in your home, the White House!

A Special Note From...
The White House
1600 Pennsylvania Avenue
Washington, D.C. 20500

Official White House Steno Pad.   Use Only Disappearing Ink.

Secret Diaries Activity!
A Day in the Life of a White House Kid!

Our Presidents

Here is a list of presidential election winners—so far. The next presidential election is in 2020.

PRESIDENT	YEARS	PARTY	PRESIDENT	YEARS	PARTY
George Washington	1789–1797	Federalist	Grover Cleveland	1885–1889	Democratic
John Adams	1797–1801	Federalist	Benjamin Harrison	1889–1893	Republican
Thomas Jefferson	1801–1809	Democratic/Republican	Grover Cleveland	1893–1897	Democratic
James Madison	1809–1817	Democratic/Republican	William McKinley	1897–1901	Republican
James Monroe	1817–1825	Democratic/Republican	Theodore Roosevelt	1901–1909	Republican
John Quincy Adams	1825–1829	Democratic/Republican	William Howard Taft	1909–1913	Republican
			Woodrow Wilson	1913–1921	Democratic
			Warren G. Harding	1921–1923	Republican
Andrew Jackson	1829–1837	Democratic	Calvin Coolidge	1923–1929	Republican
Martin Van Buren	1837–1841	Democratic	Herbert Hoover	1929–1933	Republican
William Henry Harrison	1841	Whig	Franklin D. Roosevelt	1933–1945	Democratic
John Tyler	1841–1845	Whig	Harry S. Truman	1945–1953	Democratic
James K. Polk	1845–1849	Democratic	Dwight D. Eisenhower	1953–1961	Republican
Zachary Taylor	1849–1850	Whig	John F. Kennedy	1961–1963	Democratic
Millard Fillmore	1850–1853	Whig	Lyndon B. Johnson	1963–1969	Democratic
Franklin Pierce	1853–1857	Democratic	Richard M. Nixon	1969–1974	Republican
James Buchanan	1857–1861	Democratic	Gerald R. Ford	1974–1977	Republican
Abraham Lincoln	1861–1865	Republican	James (Jimmy) Carter	1977–1981	Democratic
Andrew Johnson	1865–1869	Republican	Ronald Reagan	1981–1989	Republican
Ulysses S. Grant	1869–1877	Republican	George Bush	1989–1993	Republican
Rutherford B. Hayes	1877–1881	Republican	Bill Clinton	1993–2001	Democratic
James A. Garfield	1881	Republican	George W. Bush	2001–2009	Republican
Chester A. Arthur	1881–1885	Republican	Barack H. Obama	2009–2017	Democratic
			Donald J. Trump	2017–	Republican

Who will be next?

Presidential Elections Quiz

1. How many electoral votes are required to win an election?
- ○ A 27
- ○ B 270
- ○ C 537
- ○ D 281,421,906

2. The Tuesday after the first Monday in November is called —
- ○ A Election Day
- ○ B Thanksgiving
- ○ C Happy Birthday
- ○ D Leap Year

3. "Electors" (usually members of the major political parties) chosen from each state are called —
- ○ A Electoral college
- ○ B Electoral candidates
- ○ C Presidential candidates
- ○ D College graduates

4. What are the requirements to become president?
- ○ A Must be a natural born citizen
- ○ B Must be at least 35 years old
- ○ C Must have lived in the United States for at least 14 years
- ○ D All of these

5. Who is next in line if the president dies?
- ○ A Speaker of the House
- ○ B Vice president
- ○ C President pro tempore of the Senate
- ○ D Secretary of state

6. A document or list of signatures that makes a request of a legislative body is a —
- ○ A Caucus
- ○ B Direct primary
- ○ C Nominating convention
- ○ D Petition

7. Which symbol represents the Democratic Party?
- ○ A Elephant
- ○ B Monkey
- ○ C Donkey
- ○ D Stars and Stripes

8. Which symbol represents the Republican Party?
- ○ A Elephant
- ○ B Monkey
- ○ C Donkey
- ○ D Stars and Stripes

9. Characteristics of a population regarding its size, growth, or density are called —
- ○ A Special graphics
- ○ B Awesome graphics
- ○ C Demographics
- ○ D Shady graphics

10. Local people who work together on a campaign are called the —
- ○ A Deep roots
- ○ B Grassroots
- ○ C Ancient roots
- ○ D Root cellar

11. Other than the Democrats and Republicans, the two other political parties that have won the presidency during U.S. history are the –
- ○ A Green and Libertarian parties
- ○ B Federalist and Whig parties
- ○ C Conservative and Tory parties
- ○ D Socialist and Radical parties

12. Who was the first president to keep pets on the White House property?
- ○ A George Washington
- ○ B Thomas Jefferson
- ○ C John Adams
- ○ D Andrew Jackson

See pg. 40 for answers

37

Donald Trump: A Reality SURVIVOR!

My brother Freddy was eight years older than me. While he was in college and I was in military school, he would take me on fishing trips with his friends, and we would share in great adventures.

Freddy's passion was flying, but our father always wanted him to take over the family business. When he graduated from college, Freddy put aside his dream and came to work for my father. Unfortunately, they got into a big disagreement about some expensive new windows Freddy ordered for a real estate development, and Freddy began working as a pilot for Trans World Airlines.

After he got married, had two children, and settled into a home in Queens, New York, Freddy's life tragically turned upside-down in the 1970s. His drinking alcohol got out of control. I tried to convince him to return to the real estate business, hoping that would help settle him down.

Sadly, Freddy got divorced and quit flying because he knew his drinking was creating a danger to his passengers. By 1977, he was living with our parents and working on the maintenance crew for the Trump real estate business. I asked him to be best man in my wedding to my first wife, Ivana, hoping it would brighten his spirits.

The Trump Family

Unfortunately, Freddy died four years later. Freddy would have been an amazing peacemaker for our family and the company if he didn't have a drinking problem, because everybody loved him. When Freddy was younger, he had a free spirit, was incredibly passionate, and confidently followed his dreams.

My brother's death and difficulties in life affected me deeply. To this day, I have never drank a single drop of alcohol. I give speeches on success and tell my audiences they have to love what they do. Freddy loved to fly, and drinking got in the way.

Life is short. I remind myself to cherish every moment and tell others to do the same.

Freddy Trump

CHART MY COURSE! It is about _____ miles from Manhattan, New York, to the White House!

38

See pg. 40 for answer

Continue to Learn

BOOKS BY CAROLE MARSH

Presidential Elections: All About the Electoral Process, Campaigning, Political Parties, and Much More!

Elections! Elections! Elections! Fundamental Facts and Popular Projects for the Electoral Process!

WEBSITES

Close Up Foundation
www.closeup.org

Presidential Classroom
www.presidentialclassroom.org

Junior State of America
www.jsa.org

Washington Workshops Foundation
www.workshops.org

Global Young Innovators Initiative
https://www.envisionexperience.com/explore-our-programs/
global-young-innovators-initiative

Taking It Global
http://www.tigweb.org

Kids Voting USA
http://www.kidsvotingusa.org/

Rock the Vote
http://www.rockthevote.com/about-us/

39

Glossary

West Wing Words You Need to Know!

accountability: the need for elected officials to prove they are doing the job the people elected them to do

amendment: alteration of or addition to a bill, constitution, etc.; a change made by correction, addition, or deletion

assassinate: to murder an important person like a political figure

bicameral: legislature with two houses or chambers

bill: written proposal to change or create a new law

bipartisan: when people from two political parties work together to get something done, like passing a bill into law

bully pulpit: a public office or position of authority that lets someone speak out on any issue

bureaucrat: person who gets into office, then just does a so-so job instead of working on improvement

Cabinet: persons appointed by a head of state to head executive departments of government and act as official advisors

inauguration: formal ceremony where a person takes an oath of office

incapacitation: being unable to perform a certain act or action

incumbent: a person already in office who runs for that office again

lame duck: an incumbent office holder who has lost the election or cannot run again, but has not officially left office; "lame ducks" sometimes seem less powerful because they are soon leaving office

lobbyist: person paid to try to get bills passed for special groups

markup: a congressional committee session in which a bill is written into final form, before it is sent out to members of Congress

naturalize: the process of granting full citizenship to a person born in another country

"red tape": term that means you have to jump through a lot of hoops to get something done!

resolution: a formal statement by Congress giving its opinion or decision

underdog: candidate for office who is not believed to have much of a chance to win—but sometimes does!

Quiz Question Answers
Pg. 18: Jimmy Carter, Abraham Lincoln
Pg. 25: a-11, b-2, c-9, d-12, e-10, f-7, g-1, h-6, i-5, j-3, k-8, l-4, m-13
Pg. 27: A-3, B-5, C-4, D-2, E-1
Pg. 29: 1-D, 2-varies, 3-B, 4-C, 5-the center, 6-C, 7-1891, 8-5
Pg. 37: 1-B, 2-A, 3-A, 4-D, 5-B, 6-D, 7-C, 8-A, 9-C, 10-B, 11-B, 12-C
Pg. 38: 230